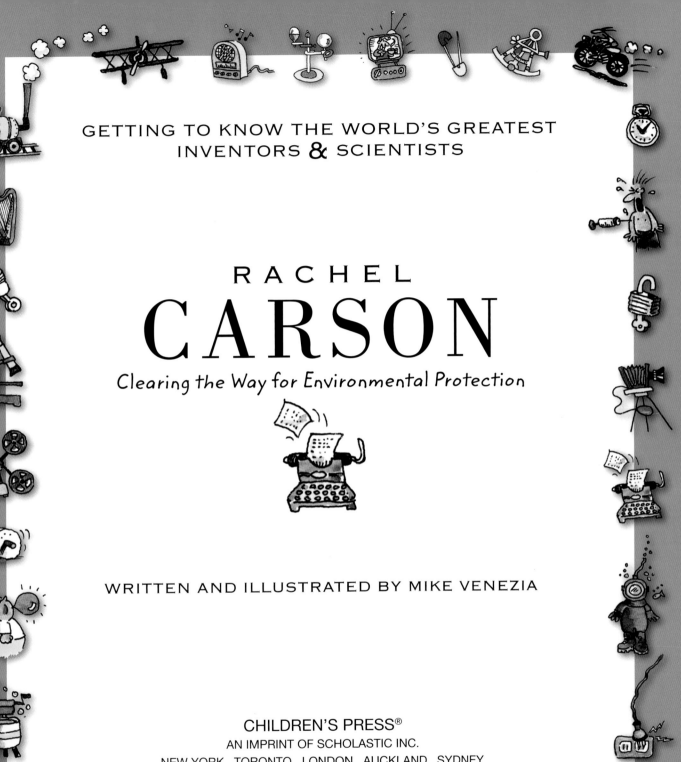

GETTING TO KNOW THE WORLD'S GREATEST
INVENTORS & SCIENTISTS

RACHEL
CARSON
Clearing the Way for Environmental Protection

WRITTEN AND ILLUSTRATED BY MIKE VENEZIA

CHILDREN'S PRESS®
AN IMPRINT OF SCHOLASTIC INC.
NEW YORK TORONTO LONDON AUCKLAND SYDNEY
MEXICO CITY NEW DELHI HONG KONG
DANBURY, CONNECTICUT

For Naomi Venezia—a super animal lover!

Reading Consultant: Nanci R. Vargus, Ed.D., Assistant Professor, School of Education, University of Indianapolis

Content Consultant: Nancy Gift, Acting Director, Rachel Carson Institute, Chatham University

Photographs © 2010: Beinecke Rare Book and Manuscript Library, Yale Collection of American Literature: 12 left, 12 right; Chatham College, Archives, Pittsburgh, PA: 31 top (Cover from *Silent Spring* by Rachel Carson (Boston: Houghton Mifflin, 1962)); Corbis Images/Bettmann: 4, 5 left, 5 right; Getty Images: 3 (Alfred Eisenstaedt), 30 (George Silk), 25 (David Woodfall); Magnum Photos/Erich Hartmann: 24, 31 bottom; National Geographic Image Collection/Melissa Farlow: 17; Penguin Group USA: 26 (*Under the Sea Wind* by Rachel Carson, © 1941 Signet Science Library); Rachel Carson Council, Inc.: 21 (Mary Frye), 8, 10, 14, 15, 22; St. Nicholas Magazine, For Boys and Girls, September, 1918, © 1918 by the Century Co.: 13; Woods Hole Oceanographic Institution: 20.

Colorist for illustrations: Andrew Day

Library of Congress Cataloging-in-Publication Data

Venezia, Mike.
  Rachel Carson : clearing the way for environmental protection / written and illustrated by Mike Venezia.
     p. cm. — (Getting to know the world's greatest inventors and scientists)
  Includes index.
  ISBN-13: 978-0-531-23704-5 (lib. bdg.) 978-0-531-20778-9 (pbk.)
  ISBN-10: 0-531-23704-4 (lib. bdg.)   0-531-20778-1 (pbk.)
  1. Carson, Rachel, 1907-1964—Juvenile literature. 2.
Biologists—United States—Biography—Juvenile literature. 3.
Environmentalists—United States—Biography—Juvenile literature. I.
Title. II. Series.

QH31.C33V46 2010
  333.95'16092—dc22
  [B]
                                     2009000345

1 2 3 4 5 6 7 8 9 10 R 19 18 17 16 15 14 13 12 11 10   62

Biologist and writer Rachel Carson, shown here photographing nature, is best known for creating awareness about the dangers of **chemical pesticides**.

Rachel Carson was born May 27, 1907, on a small farm in Springdale, Pennsylvania. When Rachel grew up, she became a **biologist** who wrote popular books about nature and science. She was a pioneer in the **environmental movement**, too. Many people think that the last book Rachel wrote, *Silent Spring*, was one of the most important books ever written about the environment.

Silent Spring, published in 1962, woke people up to the dangers of using **synthetic** pesticides across the United States and throughout the world. Synthetic pesticides are made from chemicals rather than from natural materials. Many of these poisonous chemicals were developed during World War II. They were sprayed on soldiers and their campsites to kill insects that carried and spread disease.

When chemical pesticides such as DDT were first developed, people didn't know they could be dangerous. In this 1945 photograph, a public beach is doused with DDT to kill mosquitoes and flies.

As this 1940s photograph shows, people even felt comfortable enough with DDT to spray it in a child's bedroom.

A plane sprays DDT over a forest to kill moths damaging trees in the Pacific Northwest in the early 1970s.

When the war ended in 1945, chemical **manufacturers** began to sell their products to farmers, government agencies, and everyday people. Soon pesticides such as DDT were being used all over the place—from schoolrooms to city parks and farms. These chemicals were great for getting rid of pesty mosquitoes and flies, as well as insects that damaged crops.

Rachel Carson pointed out in her book that many pesticides weren't killing just annoying insects, but birds, fish, and all kinds of animals. She found evidence that some of these chemicals were causing human illness, too.

In May 1963, Rachel was invited to Washington, D.C. There she spoke to a special committee formed by President John F. Kennedy to investigate the use of pesticides. Rachel talked about the danger of misusing tons and tons of pesticides and weed killers. Committee members were impressed with

Rachel's findings. They agreed that overuse of chemical poisons was a major problem that had been given hardly any attention.

Rachel then testified before the U.S. Congress, asking for new policies to protect human health and the environment. Her speech helped convince Congress to eventually pass important environmental-protection laws, including a nationwide ban on DDT. It was a good day for all living things on Earth!

Rachel Carson at age two (center), with her mother, sister, and brother

Rachel Carson grew up on her family's farm with her parents, an older brother and sister, and lots of pets and farm animals. The Carsons never had much money, but that didn't seem to bother Rachel a bit. As a child, she did lots of fun things that money couldn't buy.

When Rachel was very little, her mom started teaching her about the wonders of nature. Rachel spent hours exploring the woods around her

farm with her dog, Candy. She loved to study birds making their nests. She and Candy ran through fields of wildflowers and watched fish swim in the streams. Rachel later wrote that she was happiest spending time with wild birds, insects, and other animals as her friends.

Five-year-old Rachel reading a story to her dog, Candy

Rachel was also really excited about reading and writing. She said she remembered starting to read when she was still practically a baby. Her favorite books were about animals. Rachel particularly enjoyed stories like *Peter Rabbit* and *The Wind in the Willows*, books in which animals talked and had exciting and fun adventures.

Early on, Rachel realized that someone had to have thought up and written the stories she enjoyed so much. She decided it might be fun to do the same thing herself.

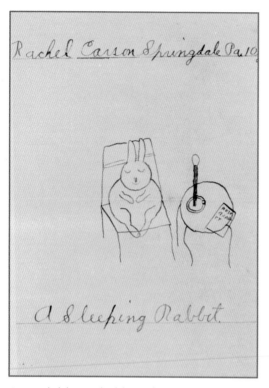

Rachel Carson Springdale Pa. 10

A Sleeping Rabbit.

As a child, Rachel loved to write and illustrate her own stories.

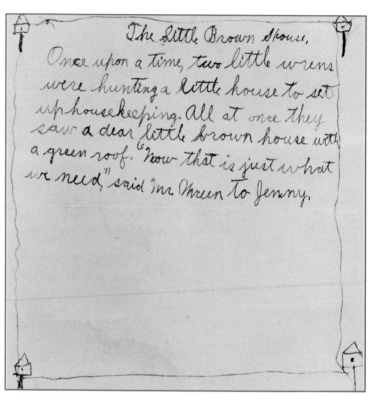

The Little Brown House.
Once upon a time, two little wrens were hunting a little house to set up housekeeping. All at once they saw a dear little brown house with a green roof. "Now that is just what we need," said Mr. Wren to Jenny.

When Rachel started school, she did very well. Her teachers thought she was polite, a good reader, and an especially good writer. Whenever Rachel had spare time, she wrote stories for her family. She often included her own illustrations, and even designed her own book covers.

When Rachel was ten years old, she sent one of her stories to *St. Nicholas*, her favorite children's magazine. *St. Nicholas* included a special section of stories by young writers. Just before her eleventh birthday, Rachel received good news. The magazine was going to publish her story!

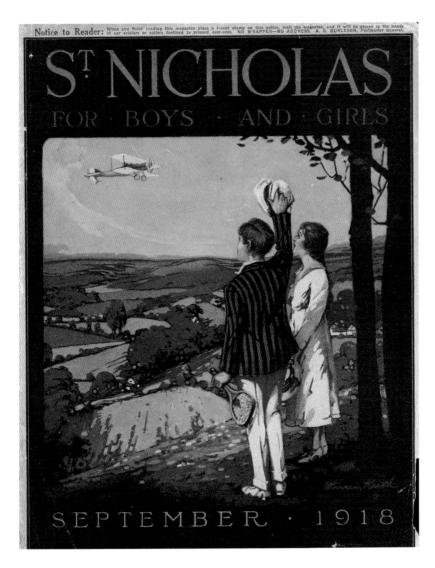

When Rachel was eleven years old, a story she wrote appeared in this edition of the children's magazine *St. Nicholas*.

Not only did the magazine print Rachel's story, it even awarded her a special honor for it. This was the beginning of Rachel's writing career. Rachel continued writing stories for *St. Nicholas* magazine, even throughout high school.

Rachel Carson at the time of her graduation from high school in 1925

Rachel (top row, second from right) played on the field-hockey team when she was in college.

After graduating from high school, Rachel attended the Pennsylvania College for Women (now Chatham College), where she studied English literature and composition. Rachel was planning to make writing her career. During her second year in college, however, something happened that changed everything. Rachel was required to take a science course. Even though she wasn't crazy about the idea, Rachel began a class in biology.

Rachel was totally surprised by how interesting the class was. She loved learning about the science of living things. As part of the class, Rachel had to **dissect** insects, frogs, and starfish. The messy job didn't bother her at all, though.

On class field trips, Rachel and her classmates learned about flowers and other plant life. Sometimes they spent the day chipping away at rocks to find ancient **fossils.** Once, Rachel was surprised to find a fish fossil when she broke open a rock. She was amazed to learn that the dry, rocky area near her college had been the bottom of a lake or ocean thousands of years earlier.

Soon, Rachel decided to take more science classes. Her main interest was **zoology,** the scientific study of animal life. She was particularly interested in creatures that lived in the sea.

Rachel was fascinated by the fish fossil she found when she broke open a rock during a college field trip. The fossil she found might have looked similar to this one (above).

Rachel had never actually been to the ocean, but she had read lots of books about the sea. One poem in particular really inspired her. On a dark, rainy night in her dorm room, Rachel read *Locksley Hall*, a poem by Alfred Lord Tennyson. The main character in this poem decides to leave his past life behind and head to the sea. One line in the poem, "For the mighty wind arises, roaring seaward, and I go," really stuck in Rachel's head. She read the line over and over, and became convinced that her life, too, would somehow be connected to the sea.

Rachel was thrilled to be invited to study at Woods Hole Marine Biology Lab in Massachusetts. This is an aerial view of the lab today.

In 1929, Rachel graduated from college at the top of her class, with a degree in biology. Because of her excellent grades, she was offered two great opportunities. First, she was invited to spend the summer at the Marine Biology Laboratory in Woods Hole, Massachusetts. Second, she was awarded a **scholarship** to further her studies at Johns Hopkins, a highly respected university in Baltimore, Maryland. These were impressive accomplishments for a woman in the 1920s.

Rachel had a great summer at Woods Hole. She got to work with marine biologists, explore sea life, and see up close, for the first time, the remarkable beauty and power of the ocean.

Rachel during her six-week stay at Woods Hole in 1929

In the fall, Rachel started graduate school at Johns Hopkins. She ended up becoming an excellent marine biologist. After receiving a master's degree, Rachel taught for a while. Then, in 1935, she got a job at the U.S. Bureau of Fisheries (later renamed the U.S. Fish and Wildlife Service), a national agency dedicated to wildlife preservation.

Rachel Carson (far right) working with fellow writers at the U.S. Bureau of Fisheries in the 1930s

It was the perfect job for Rachel. Early on, her boss gave her a special assignment. Rachel was asked to write scripts for an educational radio series about sea life. The series was called "Romance Under Water." Rachel was nervous at first. She had never written a script before. But her writing talent and her knowledge of marine biology were just the right combination. The weekly broadcasts were a big success.

Rachel adopted her grandnephew Roger in 1957. She spent a lot of time sharing nature with him. Rachel wanted all children to be able to grow up like she did—playing outside, exploring, and learning to love nature up close.

Rachel really enjoyed her new job. The only problem was that it didn't pay very much. Rachel really needed money, because her family was depending on her more and more. At various times throughout Rachel's life, her parents, brother, sister, or nieces lived with her.

Rachel loved her family and was always ready to help them. When one of her nieces died, Rachel adopted the niece's little boy, Roger. In order to make extra money, Rachel began writing articles for magazines and newspapers. Many of them were about her concern over the pollution she saw creeping into rivers and the ocean.

Rachel wrote articles about how rivers and lakes (like this one) were becoming more and more polluted as chemical companies dumped their waste into them.

Rachel's bosses appreciated her. They promoted her and gave her more responsibility. Eventually, she became the editor-in-chief of all the publications put out by the U.S. Fish and Wildlife Service.

In 1941, Rachel tried writing her first book. It was called *Under the Sea Wind*. Rachel's book was filled with interesting scientific facts about sea life and the ocean. She made sure it was written in a way that was easy for the average person to understand and enjoy.

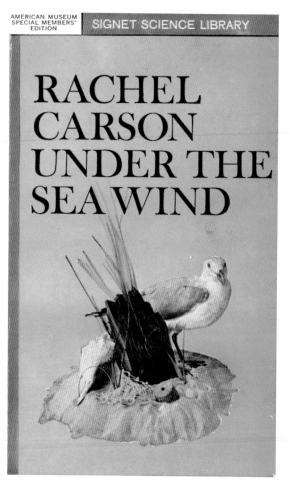

Rachel's first book, *Under the Sea Wind*, includes beautifully written descriptions of how fish and seabirds live and behave.

Rachel always did a tremendous amount of research for her books. She spent hours collecting and studying specimens along the coast. Once she went deep-sea diving, hoping to see sharks and octopuses up close. It was important to Rachel to make sure all her information was totally accurate.

Rachel was thrilled when her second book, *The Sea Around Us*, became a big best seller. She earned lots of money from the book. In 1952, Rachel decided to leave her job to work full-time on her own writing about her favorite subject: nature.

Over the years, as she collected information for her articles and books, Rachel became more concerned about the harmful effects of pollution. She learned that cities and factories everywhere were dumping too much waste into oceans and rivers. At the same time, chemical pesticides were being sprayed all over the place, and nobody seemed to realize that this was dangerous. Rachel decided she had to do something to warn people. That was when she began her most important book, *Silent Spring*.

When the heads of chemical companies heard about Rachel's book, they panicked. They were afraid people would stop buying their products. Some companies printed pamphlets and made films that said Rachel didn't really know what she was talking about. They tried to convince people that pesticides were totally safe— especially for humans.

Rachel Carson's goal wasn't to ban all pesticides. She just wanted to point out the dangers of using chemical poisons in such a widespread way. Rachel wanted chemical companies and governments to study the long-term effects of poisons more carefully and use them more responsibly. She knew that covering large areas of land with pesticides would eventually affect every living thing on Earth. She also offered suggestions for more natural ways of controlling pests, such as bringing in harmless insects that would eat the harmful ones.

Rachel wrote about how the widespread use of DDT hurt birds and other animals. For example, it caused female birds to produce eggs with shells that were so thin that the eggs couldn't survive long enough to hatch.

Sadly, Rachel Carson died of cancer in 1964, not long after her famous book was published. She lived long enough, though, to see that *Silent Spring* was starting to get people's attention. Rachel's book helped spark a whole environmental movement that eventually led to the creation of the Environmental Protection Agency.

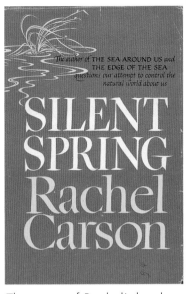

The cover of Rachel's book *Silent Spring*

In 1980, Rachel was **posthumously** awarded the Presidential Medal of Freedom.

Rachel Carson in 1962

Glossary

biologist (bye-OL-uh-jist) A scientist who studies living things

chemical pesticide (KEM-uh-kuhl PESS-tuh-side) A human-made poison that is designed to kill pests such as insects

dissect (dye-SEKT) To cut apart a dead animal in order to examine it

environmental movement (en-VYE-ruhn-MEN-tuhl MOOV-muhnt) A movement, beginning in the 1960s, in which people joined together to support the cause of protecting wildlife and the environment

fossil (FOSS-uhl) The remains or traces of an animal or plant from millions of years ago, preserved as rock

manufacturer (man-yoo-FAKT-chur-uhr) A company that produces things in large quantities

posthumously (POHST-chuh-muhss-lee) Done after one's death

scholarship (SKOL-ur-ship) An award of financial aid that a school offers to a student

synthetic (sin-THET-ik) Something that is made from chemicals rather than from materials found in nature

zoology (soh-OL-uh-jee) The science that deals with the study of animal life

Index